Sun at Midnight

Amazing Arctic Climate

By Sharon Stewart

With special thanks to:

Don Aker, Judy Bagshaw, Bob Barton, Lynn Blanche, Lynn Bryan, Margaret Carney, Maureen Dockendorf, Christine Finochio, Leslie Garrett, Gib Goodfellow, Sharon Jeroski, Deborah Kekewich, Laura Langston, Margaret Lysecki, Debora Pearson, Jeff Siamon, Sharon Siamon, Liz Stenson, Sharon Stewart, Frieda Wishinsky, Iris Zammit

Director of Publishing Mark Cobham
Publisher Anita Borovilos
Product Manager Sarah McDowell
Executive Editor Elynor Kagan
Editorial Team Chelsea Donaldson, Ann Echlin, Kathleen ffolliott, Susan Green, Geraldine Kikuta, Angelie Kim, Anne MacInnes, Milena Mazzolin, Kelly Ronan, Rena Sutton, Rebecca Vogan
Production Theresa Thomas, Zane Kaneps
Design Team David Cheung, Zena Denchik, Monica Kompter, Lisa Lapointe, Alex Li, Jennifer Stimson
Illustrators Deborah Crowle: pages 4, 8, 19t; Tina Holdcroft: pages 5, 24t, 28; Anthony Leung: pages 6, 9, 10, 11, 14, 19b, 20, 24b, 25, 26, 29
Photo Research/Permissions Karen Taylor/Alene McNeill/Barbara Welling

Picture Credits: contents Stone Allstock/Getty Images; title page Simon Fraser/Science Photo Library; 4–5 Imagestate/firstlight.ca; 7b Brian Summers/firstlight.ca; 7t Jerry Kobalenko/ firstlight.ca; 8 Tom L. McKnight/TLM Photo; 9 Stone/Getty Images; 10 © Julius/CORBIS/MAGMA; 12t © 2004 Michael DeYoung/AlaskaStock.com; 12b Image Bank/Getty Images; 13 Aurora & Quanta Productions; 14b & cover Paul Souders/ The Image Bank/Getty Images; 15l © Kennan Ward/CORBIS/MAGMA; 15r Jerry Kobalenko/firstlight.ca; 17 © Wolfgang Kaehler/CORBIS/MAGMA; 18t Courtesy of Environment Canada; 18b David Hay Jones/Photo Researchers, Inc.; 22–23 & cover Imagestate/firstlight.ca; 22i © Science Photo Library; 23il © Arjen & Jerrine Verkaik/Skyart Productions; 23ir © Arctic Photos.com; 26 © Animals, Animals; 27 © Joseph Sohm; Visions of America/CORBIS/MAGMA; 28l Image Bank/Getty Images; 28r © Ralph A. Clevenger/CORBIS/MAGMA; 30 Darwin Wiggett/firstlight.ca; 32 © Roy Corral/CORBIS/MAGMA.

ISBN: 0-13-123433-1

Printed in Canada
5 6 7 8 9 10   10 09 08 07

Contents

What Is the Arctic?

The Arctic is a large area around the North Pole. It is mostly frozen sea, but it also includes some land. Some scientists say the Arctic starts at the Arctic Circle, which is at 66°30' north **latitude.** Above this line, the Sun does not set on the longest day of the year. Others think the Arctic starts north of the **tree line.** Above the tree line, the average temperature in July is below 10°C. Trees will not grow where it is too cold.

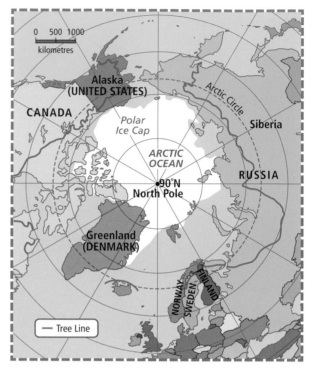

0 500 1000
kilometres

Alaska
(UNITED STATES)

CANADA

Arctic Circle

Polar
Ice Cap

Siberia

ARCTIC
OCEAN

RUSSIA

•90°N
North Pole

Greenland
(DENMARK)

NORWAY
SWEDEN
FINLAND

— Tree Line

Even though it is very cold, animals such as seals, walrus, and polar bears spend part of the year on the Arctic ice.

The Arctic Ocean

The Arctic Ocean is Earth's smallest ocean. It is up to 4000 m deep and is frozen from October to June. The polar **ice cap** is always changing. The ice cracks and heaves and breaks into sheets called floes. In summer, the edge of the ice melts near the shore but the rest of the sea stays frozen.

Earth's North Pole is located in the middle of the Arctic Ocean at 90° north latitude. If you stand at the North Pole, everywhere else in the world is south of you.

fabulous fact

Our word "Arctic" comes from *arktos*, the Greek word for "bear." This is because the Great Bear and Little Bear constellations, or star pictures, can always be seen in the Arctic sky at night. The Great Bear constellation is shown below. It contains the group of stars called the Big Dipper.

5

Why Is the Arctic Cold?

Everyone knows that the Arctic has a cold **climate.** Have you ever wondered why? The amazing fact is that both cooling *and* heating cause the unique Arctic climate.

Sun Power

The angle of the Sun's rays affects our climate. At the equator, the Sun's rays strike Earth straight on (at a 90° angle). This creates a lot of heat. In the Arctic, however, the Sun never rises more than halfway up the sky—even in summer. So the Sun's rays strike the Arctic at a lower angle. The rays give less heat. That's the main reason why the Arctic is so cold.

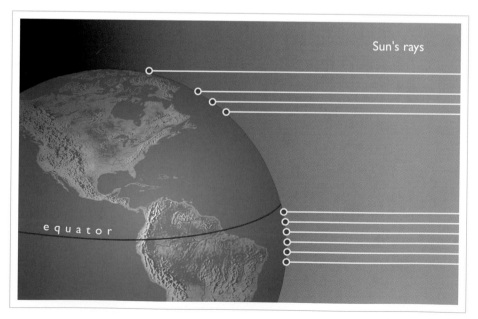

As Earth curves away from the Sun, the Sun's rays strike at lower angles. The rays that reach the Arctic are spread over a wider area and that's why they give less heat.

Clouds act like a blanket. The Arctic would be even colder if its skies were always clear.

Atmosphere and Clouds

Heat from other parts of Earth keeps the Arctic from being even colder. Warm air rises over the equator and moves north. Cool air sinks in the Arctic and moves south. In this heat exchange, lands near the equator become a little cooler and the Arctic becomes a little warmer.

The Arctic is often cloudy during the summer. These clouds affect the climate. They keep some of the Sun's rays out, but they also bounce warmth back to Earth's surface.

Arctic Shivers

Wind can make it feel colder than it really is outside. This is called the wind chill effect. It may be –20°C outside, but a light wind that blows at 10 km/h can give a wind chill of –27°C. **Frostbite** can happen at wind chills below –25°C. No wonder northerners need parkas!

El Niño

Warm water sometimes forms in the Pacific Ocean near South America. This effect is called El Niño, which means "the little boy" in Spanish. El Niño affects climates around the world. It can make the western Arctic much warmer and drier.

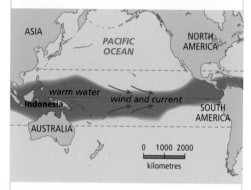

El Niño is an effect that can change climates around the world.

Ocean Currents and Rivers

Ocean currents and rivers also affect the Arctic climate. Some currents bring warm water up from the south. Others carry colder water away from the Arctic Ocean. The North Atlantic Drift is a current that brings warm water to the Arctic Ocean. It also warms the air above it.

Rivers in Canada and Russia pour warmer water into the Arctic Ocean. Like the ocean currents, this water warms the Arctic air.

The Mackenzie is Canada's longest river. It carries water from the Northwest Territories to the Arctic Ocean.

Large herds of reindeer roam the northern plains of Siberia.

Land Masses and Water

The Arctic Ocean cools the land in the summer. It also warms the land in the winter. The hottest and coldest temperatures in the Arctic are always in Siberia, Russia. This is because Siberia has a lot of land that is far from the ocean.

Antarctica Versus the Arctic

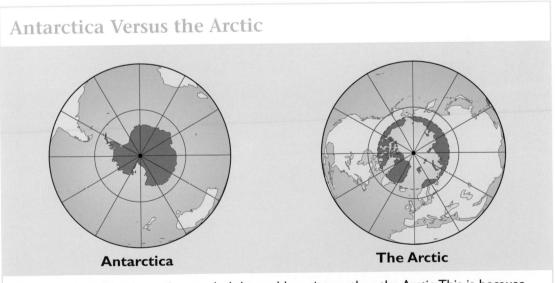

Antarctica   **The Arctic**

Antarctica is at Earth's southern pole. It has colder winters than the Arctic. This is because Antarctica has more land. The coldest temperature ever recorded on Earth was -128.6°C in the Antarctic region.

9

Snow and Ice

Snow and ice in the Arctic help keep the climate cold. The white of the snow and ice reflects almost all of the Sun's warm rays back into space. Since the Arctic has so much snow and ice, it's always losing more of the Sun's warmth than it gets. No wonder the Arctic is cold!

Sun's rays

Snow and ice reflect more of the Sun's rays than open water.

The snowmobile makes winter travel easier in Canada's Arctic.

Experiment:
Investigate Angles and Temperature

You Will Need

- 3 pieces of black paper
- scissors, tape
- 3 pieces of cardboard
- 3 thermometers
- 2 pieces of wood

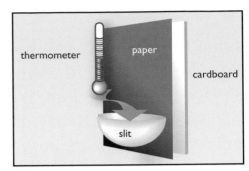

Figure 1

What to Do

1. Cut a slit near the bottom of each sheet of paper.
2. Tape each sheet to a different piece of cardboard.
3. Slip a thermometer into each slit, and tape it to the paper. (See Figure 1.)
4. When the sun is directly overhead, place one thermometer flat. Prop another one at a 45° angle. Prop the third one standing upright (0°). (See Figure 2.)
5. After about 15 minutes, check the temperature on each thermometer.

What Happens

The Sun's rays heat the thermometers differently. The thermometer that is flat (90°) represents the way the Sun's rays strike the equator. Which thermometer shows the highest temperature? Which one shows the lowest?

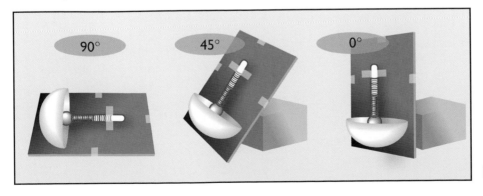

Figure 2

From Polar Night to Midnight Sun

What's the difference between climate and weather? Climate is the average weather of a place over a long time. **Weather** is what happens from day to day. There are two main types of climate in the Arctic. Near the ocean it is milder and there is more snow in winter. Farther away from the ocean it is much colder and there is less snow in winter. Some Arctic areas are really cold deserts that get less than 25 cm of **precipitation** a year.

The Arctic climate really has only two seasons, winter and summer. Spring and fall are just short periods in-between.

Alaska has a milder climate and gets more snow than Siberia.

The Canadian Arctic is very cold and does not get much snow or rain. It is sometimes called a "polar desert."

People who live in the Arctic must get used to long months of darkness. This photo was taken in the afternoon.

Where Did the Sun Go?

Arctic winters are long and cold. In some places, it starts to snow in September. Winters are dark, too. In the far north, the Sun sets in early fall and is not seen again for many months. For a while, there is a short twilight period where the sky is partially lit by the Sun. In many places, though, the long period of darkness called polar night starts in October. Without the heat from the Sun's rays, the Arctic becomes very cold. Much of the Arctic is so cold that deep layers of the soil stay frozen all year. This is known as permafrost.

Facts About Arctic Climate	
Average Winter Temperature	−34°C
Average Summer Temperature	below 10°C
Average Annual Precipitation	20 cm
Wind Speed	48–97 km/h
Last Sunset (North Pole)	about September 22
First Sunrise (North Pole)	about March 20

The Midnight Sun

At the North Pole, the Sun rises on March 21 and does not set again until September 21. Like polar night, this effect is caused by the way Earth tilts toward the Sun. Since the Sun shines day and night in the summer, the Arctic is often called "the Land of the Midnight Sun."

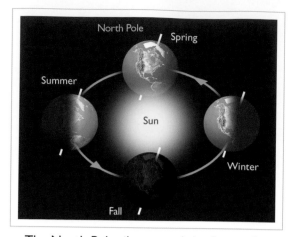

The North Pole tilts toward the Sun in the summer. During this time, the Sun stays above the horizon up to 24 hours a day.

Summer in the Arctic

Arctic summers are short and cool, and they are often cloudy. It can rain or even snow. As the edge of the sea thaws, warm air moves across the cold water. This creates fog. Over the Arctic Ocean, the temperature stays around 0°C. Over land, though, the days can be much warmer. A town in Siberia once recorded a summer temperature of 37°C!

In North America, the snow covering the **tundra** is gone by July. The top layers of permafrost melt. This creates puddles and wet mossy areas called bogs. For a few weeks, wildflowers bloom. Birds and other wild creatures give birth to their young.

Icebergs fall from Arctic glaciers in the summer. Ocean currents carry the icebergs south to the Atlantic Ocean.

14

Activity:
Investigate Your Local Climate

How hot are the summers where you live? How cold are the winters? Does it rain or snow a lot? Check Environment Canada's Web site on the Internet. Go to the library to find an atlas that shows the temperature and precipitation for your area. You could also use a travel guide.

When you have finished your research, display your findings on a chart. Compare your data with what you know about Arctic climate.

Climate Facts Data	Local Climate	Arctic Climate
Average Winter Temperature		
Average Summer Temperature		
Average Annual Precipitation		
Windy or Not Windy		
Length of Summer		
Length of Winter		
Other		

caribou calf

Baby animals are born and raised during the short Arctic summer.

Arctic hare nursing

Climate Detectives in the Arctic

Arctic weather and climate affect weather everywhere. **Meteorologists** study conditions in the Arctic to understand weather and climate around the world. Some weather scientists work in weather stations in the Arctic. Many of the stations are short-term camps on the sea ice. Others are long-term research centres.

Ways to Measure the Weather

Below are some common weather instruments and what they measure.

Weather Instrument	What It Measures
Rain Gauge	precipitation (the amount of moisture that has fallen from the sky)
Thermometer	temperature (how hot or cold it is)
Anemometer	wind speed (how fast the wind is blowing)
Wind Vane	wind direction (where the wind is blowing from)
Hygrometer	humidity (how much moisture is in the air)
Barometer	air pressure (the force of air pushing on the surface of Earth)
Sunshine Recorder	sunshine (hours of sunshine received)

The Frozen Chosen

Eureka, Alert, and Resolute Bay are some of Canada's most northern weather stations. The meteorologists who live in these places call themselves the "Frozen Chosen." For more than 50 years, scientists at these stations have observed the weather every day.

Not all weather stations need scientists. Computers run Canada's weather stations at Isachsen and Mould Bay. The Eureka station, however, has become a busy place. Some scientists go there to study Earth's atmosphere. Others study Arctic animals. Tourists also visit Eureka to learn more about the Arctic.

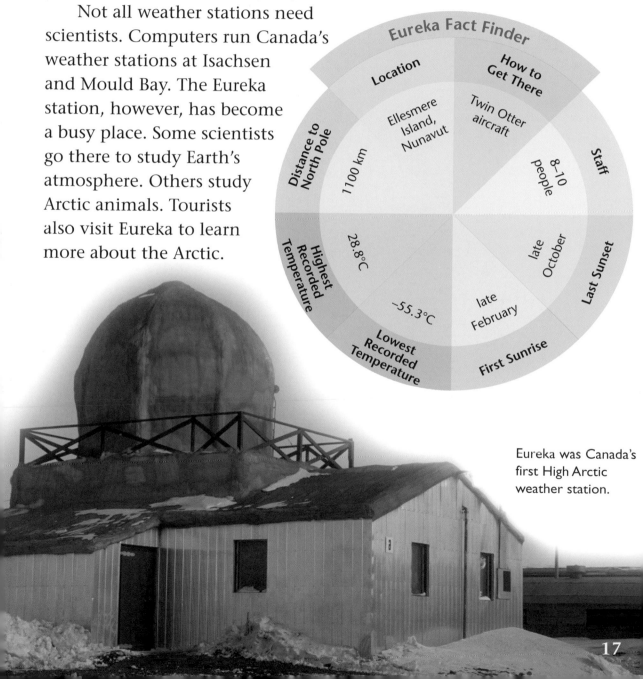

Eureka Fact Finder

Location: Ellesmere Island, Nunavut

How to Get There: Twin Otter aircraft

Staff: 8–10 people

Last Sunset: late October

First Sunrise: late February

Lowest Recorded Temperature: −55.3°C

Highest Recorded Temperature: 28.8°C

Distance to North Pole: 1100 km

Eureka was Canada's first High Arctic weather station.

17

This is a weather satellite image. It shows cloud cover over Canada's Arctic.

Buoys, Balloons, and Satellites

Arctic meteorologists gather lots of information from their weather stations. They also have other ways to collect data. Weather buoys float in the Arctic Ocean to measure temperature, **air pressure,** humidity, and winds. Weather balloons measure conditions high in the sky. Radar and weather satellites show cloud patterns, areas of rain and snow, and storms.

Scientists use balloons to send weather instruments up into the atmosphere.

Weather Forecasts and Maps

Environment Canada forecasts weather for all areas in Canada, including the Arctic. Its meteorologists can predict the weather for up to five days. Usually they are right, but the weather can still surprise us.

Weather maps show temperature, **air masses,** storm **fronts,** high and low air-pressure areas, and more. Some have isotherms—lines that show areas with the same air temperature. Others have isobars—lines that show areas with the same air pressure.

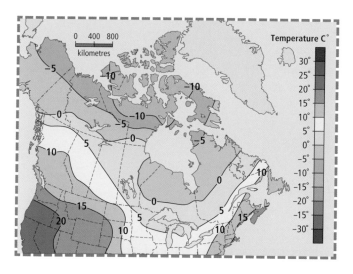

This weather map shows the temperatures for Canada and parts of the United States. Black lines, called isotherms, show areas with the same air temperature.

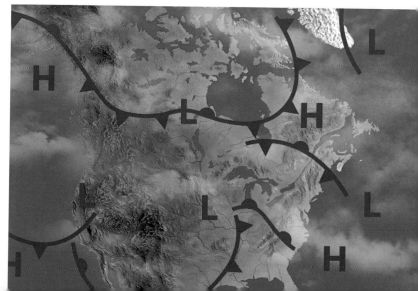

This weather map shows warm and cold fronts, and high- and low-pressure areas. High pressure brings sunny days. Low pressure brings clouds and precipitation.

Experiment:
Measure Air Pressure with a Barometer

You Will Need

- an empty coffee can or wide-mouthed jar
- plastic wrap
- a rubber band
- a straw
- tape
- a pencil
- an index card
- a ruler

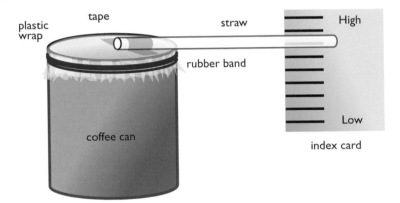

What to Do

1. Stretch the plastic wrap tightly across the top of the can and hold it in place with the rubber band.
2. Tape one end of the straw to the centre of the plastic.
3. Mark evenly spaced lines on the card. Add the labels High and Low as shown.
4. Place the can near a wall and tape the card to the wall behind it. The pointer must reach the card.
5. Mark the level of the straw on the card.
6. Record the level of the straw daily.

What Happens

Air pressure is the force of air pushing down on an area. When air heats up, it rises. This lowers the pressure of air on an area. When air cools down, it sinks and spreads out. This increases the pressure of air on an area. In the barometer, lower pressure makes the plastic bulge up, so the straw moves down. Higher air pressure makes the plastic sag, so the straw moves up.

Keeping Weather Records

Check your local newspaper or television station for weather information. Record your local weather in a weather notebook. You could use pages set up like the one shown below.

Weather Log

	Oct. 18	Oct. 19
Date		
Time	4:15 p.m.	4:30 p.m.
Temperature	15°C	13°C
Barometric Pressure	Low	Low
Humidity	High	High
Precipitation Type	None	Rain
Wind Direction	W	NW

Special Effects in the Arctic

Arctic cold and fog can create stunning special effects.

Aurora Borealis

Sometimes the Arctic sky glows with brilliant colours. These are the **aurora borealis,** or northern lights. Particles from the Sun's rays can strike gases high in Earth's atmosphere and react with its **magnetic field.** Lights then shimmer across the night sky. Yellowish-green is the most common colour. Red, blue, or purple light shows can also appear.

halo

From time to time, the Arctic night sky offers a display of shimmering lights.

Halos, Sun Dogs, and Fog-bows

Ice crystals in the Arctic air often create halos of light around the Sun. Partial halos are called arcs. When just two spots are seen on either side of the Sun, they are called Sun dogs.

Sometimes water droplets cause the special effects. Fog-bows form when Sun shines through Arctic fog. They are like rainbows without the colours.

fog-bow

Sun dogs

23

Mirages

The cold Arctic air often plays tricks with light and creates **mirages.** Cold air near the frozen ground is thicker than the air above it. The thicker air acts like a lens that bends light waves. Some mirages can make objects appear to float in the air. Other mirages can make objects seem upside down, stretched and tall, or shaped in weird ways.

fabulous fact

Cold thick Arctic air also bends sound waves toward the ground. In the right conditions, you can hear people talking up to 3 km away!

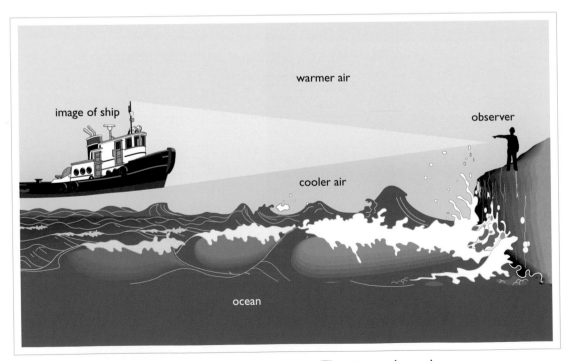

warmer air

image of ship

observer

cooler air

ocean

Cold thick air bends light rays and can create mirages. The mirage shown here makes a distant ship appear to be floating in the air.

Experiment:
Bend Light Rays

You Will Need
- a penny
- a Styrofoam cup
- water

What to Do
1. Put the penny flat on the bottom of the cup, with one edge touching the far side of the cup.
2. Place the cup so that you can see only the farthest edge of the penny.
3. Have a partner slowly pour water into the cup while you watch the penny.

What Happens
You couldn't see much of the penny in the empty cup. As you added water, you saw more and more of the penny. Why? It's because water is thicker than air and bends light rays that pass through it. Water bends the light in the same way that cold Arctic air can bend light to create a mirage.

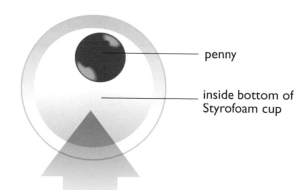

penny

inside bottom of Styrofoam cup

view cup sideways from this direction

Arctic Meltdown?

The climate of the Arctic has always changed over time. However, human actions are speeding up those changes.

The Greenhouse Effect

The Arctic climate is changing in part because of the **greenhouse effect.** Yet there would be no life on our planet without this natural process. How does it work? Gases such as carbon dioxide act like the glass in a greenhouse. That's why they are called greenhouse gases. They let the Sun's rays enter the atmosphere and warm Earth. They also trap warmth that comes from Earth's surface. Today, though, human actions are putting more and more greenhouse gases into the atmosphere. World temperatures are rising faster than ever before.

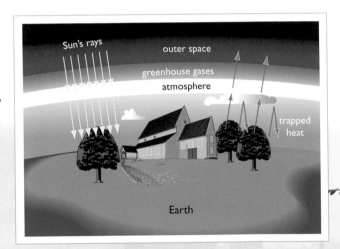

When factories burn fossil fuels, they send greenhouse gases into the atmosphere.

Global Warming

When we burn fossil fuels in cars and factories and burn down forests, do we affect the Arctic? Yes, because doing these things makes greenhouse gases. This then causes **global warming.** The more greenhouse gases we put into the air, the more Earth's temperature rises. Global warming is already starting to affect the Arctic's climate.

Guilty of Global Warming!

Human actions are adding greenhouse gases to the atmosphere. The chart on the right lists some sources of three greenhouse gases found in our air.

Greenhouse Gases	Human Sources
Carbon dioxide	• burning fossil fuels
	• cutting down and burning forests
Methane	• burning fossil fuels
	• garbage dumps
	• waste from farm animals
Nitrous oxide	• fertilizers
	• factories
	• burning things

27

Changes in Arctic Climate

The Inuit noticed Arctic warming first. They have reported melting ice, more rain, and less snow. Even the animals and birds have changed the way they act.

Scientists agree that the Arctic is getting warmer, wetter, and windier. They think that it will warm more than any other area on Earth. It may warm by as much as 7°C in winter and 5°C in summer. Already, sea ice in the Arctic Ocean is 1.3 m thinner than it was just 30 years ago.

fabulous fact

Scientists say the Arctic wasn't always cold. Thousands and thousands of years ago, tropical forests grew there!

muskox

Arctic wildlife must adapt to a changing climate. But what if the changes come too fast?

puffin

Experiment:
Use the Greenhouse Effect to Cook

You Will Need
- 2 cardboard boxes, one to fit inside the other with space left over around it
- scissors, newspaper, aluminum foil
- 1 black garbage bag
- 1 dark-coloured cooking pot with a lid
- a piece of clear plastic to cover the bigger box
- 1 piece of wood, oven mitts

What to Do
1. Line the bottom of the larger box with crumpled newspaper.
2. Set the smaller box (the cooker) inside the larger box. Pack more crumpled newspaper between them.
3. Line the inside of the cooker with foil, shiny side up. Place the folded garbage bag on the bottom.
4. Place the covered pot inside the cooker. (You could try heating a cup of water or warming a sandwich.)
5. Tape the piece of plastic in place.
6. Place the box in full Sun, using the wood to tilt it so the Sun's rays shine inside.
7. Check your cooking after 30 minutes. Use oven mitts!

What Happens
The plastic cover on your sun-powered cooker acts just like greenhouse gases in Earth's atmosphere. It lets sunlight in and traps heat.

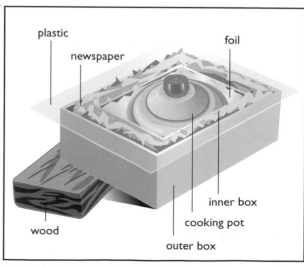

plastic

newspaper

foil

inner box

cooking pot

wood

outer box

29

Changing Arctic, Changing World?

What will a warmer Arctic mean? The Arctic Ocean will get warmer. Melting sea ice will affect animals that breed and hunt there, such as seals and polar bears. Arctic winters will be shorter and snowier. The permafrost will melt, which will cause floods and landslides. With a milder climate, the tree line will move farther north. Tundra wildlife may become endangered. A warmer Arctic will also change Earth's atmosphere, ocean currents, and weather systems.

Arctic climate is an amazing feature of our planet. No one really knows how much Earth will change because of global warming. The Arctic may already have changed forever.

If the Arctic continues to warm, the tundra may become more like a wooded bog such as this one.

Glossary

air masses   large bodies of air with the same temperature and moisture content

air pressure   the force of air that presses on an area

aurora borealis   colour displays caused by particles from the Sun striking Earth's magnetic field

climate   the average weather of a place

fronts   transition zones between two different air masses

frostbite   damage to parts of the body caused by freezing

global warming   increasing world climate temperatures caused by human actions

greenhouse effect   natural warming of Earth's climate because of gases such as carbon dioxide, methane, and nitrous oxide

ice cap   a permanent sheet of ice covering part of the land in the Arctic

latitude   distance north or south of the equator

magnetic field   an area around a magnet where its magnetic force can be felt. Earth's iron core creates a magnetic field like that of a magnet.

meteorologists   scientists who study Earth's atmosphere

mirages   false images caused by the bending of light rays in the atmosphere

precipitation   any form of water that falls from the sky

tree line   an imaginary line north of which trees do not grow

tundra   a treeless plain in the far north that has a cold, dry climate

weather   temperature, humidity, air pressure, and precipitation from day to day

Index

MAR - 2011